THE RAW
GARDEN

HELEN DUNMORE

THE RAW GARDEN

BLOODAXE BOOKS

ISBN: 1 85224 074 1

First published 1988 by
Bloodaxe Books Ltd,
P.O. Box 1SN,
Newcastle upon Tyne NE99 1SN.

Bloodaxe Books Ltd acknowledges
the financial assistance of Northern Arts.

Typesetting by Bryan Williamson, Manchester.

Printed in Great Britain by
Bell & Bain Limited, Glasgow, Scotland.

*To Mike Levine
and David Stuart*

Acknowledgements

Acknowledgements are due to the editors of the following publications where some of these poems first appeared: *Encounter, The Green Book, London Magazine, Poetry Book Society Anthology 1987/88* (Hutchinson/PBS, 1987), *Poetry Review, Prospice, Seven Years On* (Green Book Press, 1986), *Singing Brink* (Arvon Press, 1987), and the *Times Literary Supplement*. 'The Peach House' was broadcast on *Poetry Now* (BBC Radio 3).

The cover photograph is reproduced by kind permission of Will and Deni McIntyre/Science Photo Library. It shows a polarised light micrograph of crystals of AZT (azidothymidine), an antiviral drug used in the treatment of AIDS.

Contents

Seal run

The potatoes come out of the earth bright
as if waxed, shucking their compost,

and bob against the palm of my hand
like the blunt muzzles of seals swimming.

Slippy and pale in the washing-up bowl
they bask, playful, grown plump
in banks of seaweed on white sand,

seaweed hauled from brown circles
set in transparent waters off Easdale

all through the sun-fanned West Highland midnights
when the little potatoes are seeding there
to make necklaces under the mulch,
torques and amulets in their burial place.

The seals quiver, backstroking
for pure joy of it, down to the tidal
slim mouth of the loch,

they draw their lips back, their blunt whiskers
tingle at the inspout of salt water

then broaching the current they roll
off between islands and circles of oarweed.

At noon the sea-farmer
turns back his blanket of weed
and picks up potatoes like eggs
from their fly-swarming nest,

too fine for the sacks, so he puts them in boxes
and once there they smell earthy.

At noon the seals nose up the rocks
to pile there, sun-dazed,
back against belly, island on island.

and sleep, shivering like dogs
against the tug of the stream
flowing on south past Campbelltown.

The man's hands rummage about still
to find what is full-grown there.
Masts on the opposite shore ring faintly

disturbing themselves, and make him look up.
Hands down and still moving
he works on, his fingers at play blinded,
his gaze roving the ripe sea-loch.

Wild strawberries

What I get I bring home to you:
a dark handful, sweet-edged,
dissolving in one mouthful.

I bother to bring them for you
though they're so quickly over,
pulpless, sliding to juice,

a grainy rub on the tongue
and the taste's gone. If you remember
we were in the woods at wild strawberry time

and I was making a basket of dockleaves
to hold what you'd picked,
but the cold leaves unplaited themselves

and slid apart, and again unplaited themselves
until I gave up and ate wild strawberries
out of your hands for sweetness.

I lipped at your palm –
the little salt edge there,
the tang of money you'd handled.

As we stayed in the wood, hidden,
we heard the sound system below us
calling the winners at Chepstow,
faint as the breeze turned.

The sun came out on us, the shade blotches
went hazel: we heard names
bubble like stock-doves over the woods

as jockeys in stained silks gentled
those sweat-dark, shuddering horses
down to the walk.

A mortgage on a pear tree

A pear tree stands in its own maze.
It does not close its blossom all night
but holds out branchfuls of cool
wide-open flowers. Its slim leaves look black
and stir like tongues in the lamp-light.

It was here before the houses were built.
The owner grew wasteland and waited for values to rise.
The builders swerved a boundary sideways
to cup the tree in a garden. When they piled rubble
it was a soft cairn mounting the bole.

The first owner of the raw garden
came out and walked on the clay clods.
There was the pear tree, bent down
with small blunt fruits, each wide where the flower was,
shaped like a medlar, but sweet.

The ground was dense with fermenting pears,
half trodden to pulp, half eaten.
She could not walk without slipping.

Slowly she walked in her own maze,
sleepy, feeling the blood seep
down her cold fingers, down the spread branch
of veins which trails to the heart,

and remembered how she'd stood under a tree
holding out arms, with two school-friends.
It was the fainting-game,
played in the dinner-hour from pure boredom,
never recalled since. For years this was growing
to meet her, and now she's signed for her own
long mortgage over the pear tree
and is the gainer of its accrued beauty,

but when she goes into her bedroom
and draws her curtains against a spring night
the pear tree does not close its white blossom.
The flowers stay open with slim leaves flickering around them:
touched and used, they bear fruit.

A pæony truss on Sussex Place

Restless, the pæony truss tosses about
in a destructive spring wind.
Already its inner petals are white
without one moment of sun-warmed expansion.

The whole bunch of the thing looks poor
as a stout bare-legged woman in November
slopping her mules over the post office step
to cash a slip of her order book.

The wind rips round the announced site
for inner city conversion: this is the last tough
bit of the garden, with one lilac
half sheared-off and half blooming.

The AIDS ad is defaced and the Australian
lager-bright billboard smirks down
on wind-shrivelled passers-by who stayed put
to vote in the third Thatcher election.

The porch of the Elim Pentecostal Church brightens
as a woman in crimson and white suit
steps out, pins her hat down
then grasps the hands of her wind-tugged grandchildren.

Permafrost

For all frozen things –
my middle finger that whitens
from its old, ten-minute frostbite,

for black, slimy potatoes
left in the clamp,
for darkness and cold like cloths
over the cage,

for permafrost, lichen crusts
nuzzled by reindeer,
the tender balance of decades
null as a vault.

For all frozen things –
the princess and princes
staring out of their bunker
at the original wind,

for NATO survivors in nuclear moonsuits
whirled from continent to continent

like Okies in bumpy Fords
fleeing the dustbowl.

For all frozen things –
snowdrops and Christmas roses
blasted down to the germ
of their genetic zip-code.

They fly by memory –
cargo of endless winter,
clods of celeriac, chipped
turnips, lanterns at ten a.m.

in the gloom of a Finnish market-place;
flowers under glass, herring,
little wizened apples.

For all frozen things –
the nipped fish in a mess of ice,
the uncovered galleon
tossed from four centuries of memory,

for nuclear snowsuits bouncing on dust,
trapped on the rough ride of the earth's surface,
on the rough swing of its axis,

like moon-men lost on the moon
watching the earth's green flush

tremble and perish.

At Cabourg

Later my stepson will uncover a five-inch live shell
from a silted pool on the beach at St Côme. It is complete
with brass cap and a date on it: nineteen forty-three.
We'll look it up in the dictionary, take it
to show at the Musée de la Libération
– ce petit obus – but once they unwrap it
they'll drop the polite questions and scramble
full tilt for the Gendarmerie opposite.
The gendarmes will peer through its cradle of polythene
gingerly, laughing. One's at the phone
already – he gestures – 'Imagine! Let's tell them
we've got a live shell here in the Poste!'

Of course this will have happened before.
They'll have it exploded, there'll be no souvenir shell-case,
and we'll be left with our photographs
taken with a camera which turns out to be broken.

Later we'll be at the Château Fontaine-Henry
watching sleek daughters in jodhpurs come in from the fields.
I'll lie back in my green corduroy coat, and leave,
faint, to drive off through fields of sunflowers
without visiting the rooms we've paid for.
Madame will have her fausse-couche,
her intravenous injections, her glass ampoules,
in a room which is all bed
and smells of medicinal alcohol and fruit.
The children will play on the beach, a little forlornly,
in the wind which gusts up out of nowhere.

Later we'll see our friends on their lightweight bicycles
freewheeling tiredly downhill to Asnelles.
Their little son, propped up behind them
will glide past, silent, though he alone sees us.

But now we are on the beach at Cabourg,
stopped on our walk to look where the sky's whitening
over the sea beyond Dives. Now a child squawks
and races back as a wave slaps over his shorts' hem

to where a tanned woman with naked breasts
fidgets her baby's feet in the foam
straight down from the Boulevard Marcel Proust.

Ploughing the roughlands

It's not the four-wheeled drive crawler
spitting up dew and herbs,

not Dalapon followed by dressings
of dense phosphates,

nor ryegrass greening behind wire as behind glass,

not labourers wading in moonsuits
through mud gelded by paraquat –

but now, the sun-yellow, sky-blue
vehicles mount the pale chalk,

the sky bowls on the white hoops
and white breast of the roughland,

the farmer with Dutch eyes
guides forward the quick plough.

Now, flush after flush of Italian ryegrass
furs up the roughland

with its attentive, bright,
levelled-off growth –

pale monoculture
sweating off rivers of filth

fenced by the primary
colours of crawler and silo.

The land pensions

The land pensions, like rockets
shoot off from wheat with a soft yellow
flame-bulb: a rook or a man in black
flaps upwards with white messages.

On international mountains and spot markets
little commas of wheat translate.
The stony ground's pumped to a dense fire
by the flame-throwing of chemicals.
On stony ground the wheat can ignite
its long furls.

The soft rocket of land pensions flies
and is seen in Japan, covering
conical hills with its tender stars:
now it is firework time, remembrance
and melt-down of autumn chrysanthemums.

On bruised fields above Brighton
grey mould laces the wheat harvest.
The little rockets are black. Land pensions
fasten on silos elsewhere, far off.

Market men flicker and skulk like eels
half-way across earth to breed.
On thin chipped flint-and-bone land
a nitrate river laces the grey wheat
pensioning off chalk acres.

A dream of wool

Decoding a night's dreams
of sheepless uplands
the wool-merchant clings to the wool churches,

to trade with the Low Countries,
to profitable, downcast
ladies swathed in wool sleeves

whose plump, light-suffused faces
gaze from the triptychs he worships.

Sheep ticks, maggoty tails and foot-rot
enter his tally
of dense beasts, walking
with a winter's weight on their backs

through stubborn pasture
they graze to a hairsbreadth.

From the turf of the Fire Hills
the wool-merchant trawls
sheep for the marsh markets.
They fill mist with their thin cries –

circular eddies, bemusing
the buyers of mutton
from sheep too wretched to fleece.

In the right angle of morning sunshine
the aerial photographer
shoots from the blue,

decodes a landscape
of sheepless uplands
and ploughed drove roads,

decodes the airstream, the lapis lazuli
coat for many compacted skeletons
seaming the chalk by the sea.

New crops

O engines
flying over the light, barren
as shuttles, thrown over a huge
woof

crossply
of hedgeless snail tracks,
you are so high,

you've felled the damp crevices
you've felled the boulder-strewn meadow
the lichen
the strong plum tree.

O engines
swaying your rubber batons
on pods, on ripe lupins,
on a chameleon terrace
of greenlessness,

you're withdrawn from a sea
of harvests, you're the foreshore

of soaked soil leaching
undrinkable streams.

Shadows of my mother against a wall

The wood-pigeon rolls soft notes off its breast
in a tree which grows by a fence.
The smell of creosote,
easy as wild gum
oozing from tree boles
keeps me awake. A thunderstorm
heckles the air.

I step into a bedroom
pungent with child's sleep,
and lift the potty and pile of picture books
so my large shadow
crosses his eyes.

Sometimes at night, expectant,
I think I see the shadow of my mother
bridge a small house of enormous rooms.
Here are white, palpable walls
and stories of my grandmother:
the old hours of tenderness I missed.

Air layering

The rain was falling down in slow pulses
between the horse-chestnuts, as if it would set root there.

It was a slate-grey May evening
luminous with new leaves.
I was at a talk on the appearances of Our Lady
these past five years at Medjugorje.
We sat in a small room in the Presbytery:
the flow of the video scratched, the raindrop
brimmed its meniscus upon the window
from slant runnel to sill.

Later I watched a programme on air layering.
The round rootball steadied itself
high as a chaffinch nest, and then deftly
the gardener severed the new plant.
She knew its wounded stem would have made roots there.

The cherry stump

Years ago friends had a cherry tree,
big and dark in their front garden.
For one week in each year it flashed white
and for the rest did nothing
but breed dark in through the window.

It was badly planted, too close.
Its dirty bark scratted the guests' clothes,
its twigs brushed the gatepost.

They cut the tree down and the small bare
garden was bright, the windows were oblong,
not shifting lozenges beating back green.

They left a sudden stump and a frill of sawdust.
They had no choice but to poison the stump:
the tree would grow back on them, it must
rise up somehow, throwing out suckers.
Its life would snake up.

A big dark cherry like that, shaking itself –
it's not enough that you cut it to earth.
It has to be tracked through the soil by its roots
and where it is found, smoked out.

The argument

It was too hot, that was the argument.
I had to walk a mile with my feet flaming
from brown sandals and sun.

Now the draggling shade of the privet made me to dawdle,
now soft tarmac had to be crossed.
I was lugging an old school-bag –

it was so hot the world was agape with it.
One limp rose fell as I passed.

An old witch sat in her front garden
under the spokes of a black umbrella
lashed to her kitchen chair.
God was in my feet as I fled past her.

Everyone I knew was so far away.
The yellow glob of my ice cream melted and spread.
I bought it with huge pennies, held up.
'A big one this time!' the man said,
so I ate on though it cloyed me.
It was for fetching the bread
one endless morning before Bank Holiday.

I was too young, that was the argument,
and had to propitiate everyone:
the man with the stroke, and the burnt lady
whose bared, magical teeth made me
smile if I could –
Oh the cowardice of my childhood!

The peach house

The dry glasshouse is almost empty.
A few pungent geraniums with lost markings
lean in their pots.

It is nothing but a cropping place for sun
on cold Northumbrian July days.

The little girl, fresh from suburbia,
cannot believe in the peaches she finds here.
They are green and furry as monkeys –
she picks them and drops them.

All the same they are matched to the word peach
and must mean more than she sees. She will post them
unripe, in a tiny envelope
to her eight-year-old class-mates, and write
carefully in the ruled-up spaces:
'Where we are the place is a palace.'

Artichokes in Lindisfarne garden

Grey rain batted the low
island cramped over with holiness,

but later in the dry monastery garden
there was a forest of artichokes
planted up silver and tall
behind the medicinal poppies.

A donkey would eat them, lipping
their strong tips back to the heart,
then cough the choke up and bray

over the arched stones which have kept warm
and the tide on the causeway,

and its voice would be comic or sad
as you take such pleatings of silence –
a donkey rubbing itself in the monks' garden.

But the artichokes were worth money to see:
upright and helmeted as virtue
yet savage as Vikings with their long spines.

You could no more imagine cutting one down
than stewing the rank flesh of the donkey
while all the time it would bray, and the artichokes
keep up a rustle between them.

The pale tussocks of sea-pinks went zigzagging away
where the ground was untended and hollows
suddenly cupped sun. Now it was warm
to lie down there and doze to the hesitant rasp
of a hoe on the light soil held down by artichokes.

Splitting the aquilegia

I was looking to thicken my garden.
My neighbour said he would give me
a piece of his aquilegia which grew everywhere
and set root easy as walking.
When I was next out in the garden
I found the clod of it, clean-sliced, in the grass.

I put it in quickly, stood up
like the daisies children stick into mud-pats,
and it huddled to itself, wilting.

But the cleaving of its roots did not kill it.
Its curly ornate flowers sprang up so commonly
they would have choked everything.
Now, halved and roughly transported with black
bin liner wrapped at its roots, it is feeling its way
through the tense walls of the new garden.

An ecstatic preacher

He brought sermons –
frictions of air and breath
blithely pursuing song
in the dust of a hedge bottom.

In Germany the preacher ate Himmel und Erde
beside a river brimming with winter
then bowed down to Bavarian Calvaries,
the dancing of angels
ashed to the point of a pin.

The green river flooded at Innsbruck.
The water touched the feet of the preacher.
He wore dark suits, the good man,
and drank milk in the evenings, cow-warm,
and prayed to the Virgin
of black wood, thumbed over with kisses,
and prayed for the rare feast-day
when milk drops spring from her breasts, and spray
hazes her blue dress.

A meditation on the glasshouses

The bald glasshouses stretch here for miles.
For miles air-vents open like wings.

This is the land of reflections, of heat
flagging from mirror to mirror. Here cloches
force on the fruit by weeks, while pulses
of light run down the chain of glasshouses
and blind the visitors this Good Friday.

The daffodil pickers are spring-white.
Their neat heads in a fuzz of sun
stoop to the buds, make leafless
bunches of ten for Easter.

A white thumb touches the peat
but makes no print. This is the soil-less
Eden of glasshouses, heat-stunned.

The haunting of Epworth

*Epworth Rectory was the childhood home of John Wesley. In December 1716
the house was possessed by a poltergeist; after many unsuccessful attempts at
exorcism the spirit, nicknamed 'Old Jeffery' by the little Wesley girls, left of
its own accord.*

Old Jeffery begins his night music.
The girls, sheathed in their brick skin,
giggle with terror. The boys are all gone
out to the world, 'continually sinning',
their graces exotic and paid for.

Old Jeffery rummages pitchforks
up the back chimney. The girls
open the doors to troops of exorcists
who plod back over the Isle of Axeholme
balked by the house. The scrimmage
of iron, shattering windows, and brickwork
chipped away daily is birdsong
morning and evening, or sunlight
into their unsunned lives.

Old Jeffery tires of the house slowly.
He knocks the back of the connubial bed
where nineteen Wesleys, engendered in artlessness
swarm, little ghosts of themselves.
The girls learn to whistle his music.

The house bangs like a side-drum
as Old Jeffery goes out of it. Daughters
in white wrappers mount to the windows, sons
coming from school make notes – the wildness
goes out towards Epworth and leaves nothing
but the bald house straining on tiptoe
after its ghost.

Preaching at Gwennap

Gwennap Pit is a natural amphitheatre in
Cornwall, where John Wesley preached.

Preaching at Gwennap, silk
ribbons unrolling far off,
the unteachable turquoise and green
coast dropping far off,

preaching at Gwennap, where thermals revolve
to the bare lip, where granite
breaks its uneasy backbone,
where a great natural theatre, cut
to a hairsbreadth, sends back each cadence,

preaching at Gwennap to a child asleep
while the wide plain murmurs, and prayers
ply on the void, tendered like cords
over the pit's brim.
                  Off to one side
a horse itches and dreams. Its saddle
comes open, stitch after stitch,

while the tired horse, standing for hours
flicks flies from its arse
and eats through the transfiguration –
old sobersides
mildly eschewing more light.

On circuit from Heptonstall Chapel

*' 'Tis not everyone could bear these things, but I bless God, my wife is less
concerned with suffering them than I in writing them.'*
(Samuel Wesley, father of John Wesley,
writing of his wife Susanna.)

The mare with her short legs heavily mud-caked
plods, her head down
over the unearthly grasses,
the burning salt-marshes,

through sharp-sided marram and mace
with the rim of the tide's eyelid
out to the right.

The reed-cutters go home
whistling sharply, crab-wise
beneath their dense burdens,

the man on the mare weighs heavy, his broadcloth
shiny and worn, his boots dangling
six inches from ground.
He clenches his buttocks to ease them,
shifts Bible and meat,

thinks of the congregation
gathered beyond town,
wind-whipped, looking for warm
words from his dazed lips.

No brand from the burning;
a thick man with a day's travel
caked on him like salt,

a preacher, one of those scattered like thistle
from the many-angled home chapel
facing all ways on its slabbed upland.

B

Olive in a blue dress – 1946

Olive in a blue dress,
the wavy lines of her dress
blue and white under the limes.

The cameras turn and Olive's black hair
rumples like lime leaves in May air
and her smooth arm hurling a flower
beckons us in – look, this is Olive
who wore dresses in colour

and this the corner of sunlight
where boys in rough costume took bites
of dough-cake offered by Olive's Mum,

and this the film set where Olive and boys
and lime leaves shimmer under the toy
gantries, under the lights and cables of cameras.

The bare field on one side
rushes away into oblivion, tried
once and then cut – clover and bees nodding
and white clouds bowling on the horizon.

Jet trails like spider webs spread.
The boys look up and their heads
spin, faces graceless and blinking
while Olive eases her skirt down her calves.

The boys all shout something
while cameras whirr, faces set stern
and black and white shadows
steal poignancy into the film can.

A pre-war poem: the first act
June branches shuffling, the splat
of bird-lime. Little Olive at home

streaks into a municipal swimming bath
in her pink crinkle costume that hides half

the pimple of six-year-old nipples,
and puffs with her eyes burning
four yards through dazzling chlorinate blue, learning
to swim, shrieking at Dad to come in.

Now, Olive in a blue dress
the wavy lines of her dress
black and white under the limes,

leans back between two men's arms
so her flowery flesh and the harm
they're all saved from, leak onto the film.

US 1st Division Airborne Ranger at rest in Honduras

The long arm hangs flat to his lap.
The relaxed wrist-joint is tender, shade-
cupped at the base of the thumb.

That long, drab line of American cloth,
those flat brows knitting a crux,
the close-shaven scalp, cheeks, jawbone and lips

rest in abeyance here, solid impermanence
like the stopped breath of a runner swathed up
in tinfoil bodybag, back from the front.

He rests, coloured like August foliage and earth
when the wheat's cropped, and the massive harvesters
go out on hire elsewhere,

his single-lens perspex eyeshield pushed up, denting
the folds of his skull stubble, his cap
shading his eyes which are already shaded
by bone. His pupils are shuttered,
the lenses widening inwards,
notions of a paling behind them.

One more for the beautiful table

Dense slabs of braided-up lupins –
someone's embroidery – Nan,
liking the blue,

one more for the beautiful table
with roses and handkerchiefs, seams
on the web of fifty five-year-olds' life-spans.

New, tough little stitches
run on the torn
wedding head-dresses.
No one can count them
back to the far-off
ghosts of the children's conceptions.

Those party days:

one more for the beautiful table

the extinction of breath in a sash.

What looks and surprises!
Nan on her bad legs
resumes the filminess of petals
and quotes blood pricks and blood stains

faded to mauve and to white and to crisp
brown drifts beneath bare sepals –

look, they have washed out.

Lambkin

A poem in mother dialect

That's better, he says, he says
that's better.

Dense slabs of braided-up lupins –
someone's embroidery – Nan,
liking the blue,

Oh you're a tinker, that's what you are,
a little tinker, a tinker, that's what you are.

One more for the beautiful table
with roses and handkerchiefs, seams
on the web of fifty five-year-olds' life-spans.

Come on now, come on, come on now,
come on, come on, come on now,

new tough little stitches
run on the torn
wedding head-dresses.
The children count them
back to the far-off
ghosts of their own conceptions.

Oh you like that, I know, yes,
you kick those legs, you kick them,
you kick those fat legs then.

Those party days

one more for the beautiful table

set out in the hall.

You mustn't have any tears, you're my good boy
aren't you my little good boy.

What looks and surprises!
Nan on her bad legs
resumes the filminess of petals,

she'll leave it to Carlie
her bad spice.

Let's wipe those tears, let's wipe off all those tears.
That's better, he says, he says
that's right.

She quotes blood pricks and bloodstains
faded to mauve and to white and to crisp
brown drifts beneath bare sepals –

look, they have washed out.

The green recording light falters
as if picking up voices

it's pure noise grain and nothing more human.
It's all right lambkin I've got you I've got you.

In Empire

My daughter Sally moved in Empire seven years ago. That was before people became desperate to get in. Her husband Baines was a prudent man. Sally used to come and visit me regularly, even though I was living out there, and most people in Empire would not do that. I was still in the same house that Sally had grown up in. It was in what we used to call a good neighbourhood, but whatever the goodness was, it was shrinking like a puddle in the sun. Once I'd known almost everyone in the surrounding roads and crescents and avenues, by sight at least, if not to talk to. Sally had grown up with their children. We'd invite each other in at Christmas-time.

Suddenly it seemed that all those people were not there any more. The FOR SALE boards had been stuck in every garden for months, but it was no use: you couldn't sell them. There were people waiting to move in without buying. There was noise on the streets, loud noise. People crying, heels going by fast, fights. There were piles of rubbish under the privet, which grew out of shape, tall and flowering.

Baines began to tell Sally that it was too risky for her to drive over with the children, even though of course they had Armaflex on the car by then. But Sally did come, first once a week, then twice a month, then less often.

One Sunday they all came over together. It was a hot, cloudy, close day, and I had put the paddling pool out in the garden for Mel and Royston, but Baines would not let them go out of the house. Kidnapping had started, although so far only in London and the big cities. Sally was tired out, and the children were restless, irritable, impossible to amuse. It was a relief when they went, and I could start clearing up the mess from the spoilt day we'd all had.

Baines telephoned me later. Sally was in bed, she had been sick. Luckily the children had fallen asleep almost as soon as they drove off, so they hadn't seen anything.

Of course nobody would ever stop on the journey between our district and Empire. Baines took one of the stretches of motorway which was still passable. It would bring him within a mile of Empire. But as he slowed down on the slip road off the motorway, he saw a bundle of people step out from the banks and fan all over the road. He didn't stop, but he slowed. He couldn't help it, he said, it was pure reaction. The tyres were Armaflexed, so he wasn't too worried. He had spent a lot of money on that Venturer.

Sally shrank back in her seat, because you can't help doing that when those faces moon up to you against the windows, laughing at you. Baines kept moving through, nudging his way, not looking to either side. He was trying to think what he'd do if there was another ambush up ahead. Baines did not tell me much about what happened next, but Sally told me, a few days later, when I was helping her to stake delphiniums in the long herbaceous border in Empire. They prize such borders in Empire. I have always loved them myself, though they went out of fashion for many years. They were too labour-intensive. But that doesn't matter now. We watch the accredited daily workers move up and down, sober and skilful, glad to be safely within Empire. They have to go out there at night, of course. Sally likes to do a bit of gardening. It helps her to relax.

She told me that there was a girl of about twenty, with fleecy, glistening blonde hair, like a child's hair. She was in front of their car, just standing there as it came on towards her. She had a baby in her arms, a little one, not more than two months, Sally thought. Sally is still at the stage where she can tell babies' ages to the month. She speaks the mother dialect. The girl smiled at Sally, then she put the baby down in the path of the car, and stepped neatly aside. She skipped, almost, Sally said.

Baines drove over it. Well, Sally said that the wheels couldn't have gone over the baby, not the wheels themselves. Baines zigzagged a little, as much as was safe, so that the car would go over the baby, but not the wheels. Or so she said. Anyway, the baby disappeared, and as they drove forward the knot of people in front and to the side of them melted away as they ran around to the back of the Venturer to see what had become of the baby.

It eased my mind a little when Sally told me that they had done that. At least they had not thought of anything else but their baby. But what will they think of next time?

Baines accelerated, got off the slip road and safely into Empire, with the children still sleeping in the back.

After that he wouldn't let Sally come at all. A few months later they found me a place in Empire. I do the babysitting patrol, ten p.m. until 6 a.m. I am armed, in spite of the perimeter shock section and the guard towers. In return for this I have a small room, a semi-basement, but it looks out over the garden. It was only because of Baines and Sally that I got the room at all, since everyone wants to be in Empire now, and unless you've got something serious to offer, there is no chance.

I help Sally with the children when she has finished work, and I like to work in the garden, especially in the herbaceous borders. The best time is very early in the morning, after I finish my patrol, but before the accredited workers are allowed in. I don't need much sleep. I have got to know the plants well. I look out for anything new: a variegation of colour or shading. It doesn't often occur with perennials, but sometimes I find a plant which I can breed from. Sally doesn't like the way I try to develop these sports. She likes the generations to breed true, parent to child, parent to child, replicating themselves. It's understandable, I suppose.

At the resurrection
(after Stanley Spencer)

We picture gentler animals stopping to paw
the soil where we rise up. Our curious flesh
gleams softly like freshly turned roots.
The rabbit's a stranger to us by the unstitching
of genes through thousands of years' breeding.

How peeled and soft-skinned we'll look in the sun!
like hazelnuts plump in the dark
or sweet chestnuts sheathed round with spines
until the air hardens them.

The sky will be blue as a bolt
of Victorian air-blue, the sun butter-coloured,
the earth shouldering its way buoyantly.
We come back to earth where nothing's preserved
but what has sunk back and died as we did.

The earth's brown crumb is soft after frost
and ready for planting.
The rabbits lift up their heads
feeling the light tremors under them lengthen
and the crust heave as new bodies slip through it
shedding their wet, rag-patterned gleam
like fish in the iridescent first seconds of landing.

Dublin 1971

The grass looks different in another country.
By a shade more or a shade less, it startles
as love does in the sharply-tinged landscape
of sixteen to eighteen. When it is burnt
midsummer and lovers have learned to make love
with scarcely a word said, then they see nothing
but what is closest: an eyelash tonight,
the slow spread of a sweat stain,
the shoe-sole of the other as he walks off
watched from the mattress.

The top deck of the bus babbles with diplomats'
children returning from school, their language
an overcast August sky which can't clear.
Each syllable melting to static
troubles the ears of strangers, no stranger
but less sure than the slick-limbed children.
With one silvery, tarnishing ring between them
they walk barefoot past the Martello tower
at Sandymount, and wish the sea clearer,
the sun for once dazzling, fledged
from its wet summer nest of cloud-strips.

They make cakes of apple peel and arrowroot
and hear the shrieks of bold, bad seven-year-old Seamus
who holds the pavement till gone midnight
for all his mother's forlorn calling.
The freedom of no one related for thousands of miles,
the ferry forever going backward and forward
from rain runnel to drain cover...

The grass looks different in another country,
sudden and fresh, waving, unfurling
the last morning they see it, as they go down
to grey Dun Laoghaire by taxi.
They watch the slate rain coming in eastward
pleating the sea not swum in,
blotting the Ballsbridge house with its soft sheets
put out in the air to sweeten.

Fallen asleep

Sleep balls my eyelids like a rough thumb:
I'm close as rootlet to peat.

It is the gross fishmonger of King Street
hosing the day's ammoniac slab.
It will not keep.

Sleep, the scarf binding me,
tabbing the days done.
Here we confess each other
in darkness, stammering.

The hard-hearted husband

'Has she gone then?' they asked,
stepping round the back of the house
whose cat skulked in the grass.

She'd left pegs dropped in the bean-row,
and a mauve terrycloth babygrow
stirred on the line as I passed.

Her damsons were ripe and her sage was in flower,
her roses tilted from last night's downpour,
her sweetpeas and sunflowers leaned anywhere.

'She got sick of it, then,' they guessed,
and wondered if the torn-up paper
might be worth reading, might be a letter.

'It was the bills got her,' they knew,
seeing brown envelopes sheafed with the white
in a jar on the curtainless windowsill,

some of them sealed still, as if she was through
with trying to pay, and would sit, chilled,
ruffling and arranging them like flowers
in the long dusks while the kids slept upstairs.

The plaster was thick with her shadows,
damp and ready to show
how she lived there and lay fallow

and how she stood at her window
and watched tall pylons stride down the slope
sizzling faintly, stepping away
as she now suddenly goes,

too stubborn to be ghosted at thirty.
She will not haunt here. She picks up her dirty
warm children and takes them

down to the gate which she lifts as it whines
and sets going a thin cry in her.
He was hard-hearted and no good to her
they say now, grasping the chance to be kind.

The old friends

After the welcome, the facts.
Your children who are no longer children
ignore us. They push through the kitchen,
their tight-jeaned buttocks butting our chair-backs,

and your ten-year-old daughter's turned ugly. Rat-fair,
watching you, Daddy, she uses long words
where short ones would do, wishes that we were not here –
she'll read too many books, haunt libraries, suffer...

I go out to look at your garden
and watch your hands move among leaves,
tinkering, clearing off weeds.
You speak of it as you spoke of the children
years back: a luminous burden

tying you, tiding you over
the numb years of your mid-forties.
Your job marks time, and the bliss
of casual motherhood's gone altogether.

You see us off at the lane-end, sun in the frown
gilding your face. The children are nowhere.
No matter how long I crane backward, or peer
at the dark hedge where your coat's brown
against brown, your face white as the frost,
I catch nothing of you.

Paul and the jockey

He looks closely at signs, posters,
arrows to the Stubbs exhibition, posies
of dapper American girls

and matrons from Wiltshire and Gloucestershire
whose seamless daughters
measure up pictures, daring the frames
to leap off and make an apocalypse
of the noon hour on Friday.

Paul drifts to the gallery shop
and waits at the print counter.
People elbow and eddy around him
and tread on his summer Green
Flash trainers, tidemarked with rain.

He chooses two postcards
and slips them tenderly
into his anorak zip-pocket –
little arrowheads
to swell the bedroom wall evidence
of past forays.

He gauges the restaurant's
warm, folded costliness,
its air voluminous with chatter,

then pushes back tendrils
of damp, soft hair, tugs up his collar
and strikes out like a water-walker
into the free blue gallery spaces
billowing from the seams of canvases.

He examines a black horse
with its fine tracing of tack
and jockey in pink and gold
sitting above his master like sunrise.

Behind Paul, shire intimates count off
horseflesh in twelve languages
and covet slits of the green landscape

while Patrick Connolly, up,
keeps his knees like a spring
on the tense racehorse.

The sober jockey, lightboned as Paul,
eases the exotic creature from trembling
while on the horizon a flick of lightning
mirrors the taut reins.

Paul fumbles his scored catalogue
and lets its pages flop back
on the old names. It's that
horse gleaming like rain which moves
his fingers. The fine web of the canvas blooms
with sudden downpours.

At Wall-town Crags

Four fifty-year-old Americans patrol the wall.
Two women in trouser-suits, slack-buttocked, intimate,
smile at strangers after their farm breakfast
while two men josh as they load up more film.

Myrtle and Claud are insiders, fresh
from the bright stores and quarters at Lakenheath
where their boy Calvin and all the fine
young men lounge, loose-limbed with readiness.

At Housesteads they trace grainstores
and put bare fingers in carving –
graffiti of debts, likelihoods, postings,
solid to the palm as plums.
They edge sideways, rustling translations.

'Must've been cold for them here.'
'Feels kind of dark, too.' No chance to stand up
sharp as a pin and be counted miles off.

Thin wind combs down a tarn.
They hear the ringing of masts at Mystic,
they see the red stems of the dogwood
pattern the sides of white houses.

A legion got lost in the drizzle
at fifty paces, but you could still feel its
boot-throbs diffuse through the bog-cotton.
Arnie soothes his friend down. The light's useless.
They'll fix the lens cap, spend time with the girls.

Myrtle and Alice lean forward, soft-rumped
over the camp plan, murmuring mild
gobbets of fact. In name only, they're wild
for Q Florus Maternus. They too push coins in
shrines and make their local dedications.

They spread out a Black Watch blanket
in the least damp spot. When the ground quakes
from old disturbances, locked miles down,
they shake out dry picnic crumbs.

Myrtle and Alice lower themselves slowly.
Mute, stone-walled fields slide
under a sunless, quick-moving sky –
a quenched landscape, soaked till it sucks
their careless fingers, trailed off the rug.
                              Brigantia perhaps
fusing with Mithras, smiles from the shrines
which thank and beseech luck.

When they got to the camp it was dark
and as they slowed for the guard
little blowing lamps flocked to their coach
so Myrtle nearly cried out, though Claud said it was best
to look elsewhere. Calvin had written them
'Act like you don't see anything.'

A clot of bodies, faces turned up whitely,
with round dark mouths moving in them. She guessed
some would be women. They might have been singing
but the coach's sound system drowned them.

Later, when they were within,
touring the squash courts and cinema
Cal said, 'Don't judge the country
by them. Wait'll you meet Lisa!'

Four fifty-year-old Americans patrol the Wall.
Myrtle and Arnie, Alice and Claud,
out of their couples whose flesh made
Calvin and all the fine boys.
They've checked out Housesteads, Corstopitum,
and now at Wall-town Crags they're alone
sounding the air with long vowels.
Even when they think it's still
they feel some wind troubling the harebells,
and Claud looks sideways, seeing despite himself
the bulge where Alice's corset digs in
her soft flesh and hampers her smiles.

St Bonaventure's in a snowstorm

A cold morning, dusky with falling snow.
I come into the porch
and shut the mirror-glazed doors quickly.
The church air, in its casing of stone
stays warm. Today there's the rare
blizzard of Bristol winters: one in five years
elating and fierce as this.

A weekday Mass, with twenty or thirty
packed into balaclavas and scarves. Only a slip
of each face shows, lips moving, eyes closed.
Snow clods unfuse slowly, and drops gather.

The church that was green and crimson
and swagged with garlands for Christmas
is plain now, sunk back
onto the bare pulse of the Mass.

Light backs on itself, fans upward
from earth to the thick sky.
It stops at the stained-glass windows
and leaves them solid as paint blocks.

A pair of stiff little altar boys
walks up and down. The heat-loving cat
stirs on her shelf, yawns, gleams
round with her green glances.

When I come out the snow's dizzying,
vivid with colour, as if each particle
shaken, gives off crimson and green
to where I stand at the base
of down-funnelling snowflakes.

But I adjust from the church dark
into the city landscape beaten to white
sheets, jewel-like sheathed
stems bursting from snow-crusts

for half a morning and then thaw blurs it.
A lorry, its diesel unwaxed,
thrashes through slush, unevenly loaded
with frozen, opaque purple and green cabbages.

Malta

The sea's a featureless blaze.
On photographs nothing comes out
but glare, with that scarlet-rimmed fishing boat
far-off, lost to the lens.

At noon a stiff-legged tourist in shorts
steps, camera poised. He's stilted
as a flamingo, pink-limbed.

Icons of Malta gather around him.
He sweats as a procession passes
and women with church-dark faces
brush him as if he were air.

He holds a white crocheted dress
to give to his twelve-year-old daughter
who moons in the apartment, sun-sore.
The sky's tight as a drum, hard
to breathe in, hard to walk under.

He would not buy 'bikini for daughter'
though the man pressed him, with plump fingers
spreading out scraps of blue cotton.

Let her stay young, let her know nothing.
Let her body remain skimpy and sudden.
His wife builds arches of silence over her
new breasts and packets of tampons marked 'slender'.
At nights, when they think she's asleep,
they ache in the same places
but never louder than in a whisper.

He watches more women melt into a porch.
Their white, still laundry flags from window to window
while they are absent, their balconies blank.

At six o'clock, when he comes home and snicks
his key in the lock so softly neither will catch it
he hears one of them laugh.
They are secret in the kitchen, talking of nothing,
strangers whom anyone might love.

Candlemas

Snowdrops, Mary's tapers,
barely alight in the grey shadows,

Candlemas in a wet February,
the soil clodded and frostless,
the quick blue shadows of snowlight again missed.

The church candles' mass
yellow as mothering bee cells,
melts to soft puddles of wax,

the snowdrops, with crisp ruffs
and green spikes clearing the leaf debris

are an unseen nebula
caught by a swinging telescope,

white tapers
blooming in structureless dusk.

Pilgrims

Let us think that we are pilgrims
in furs on this bleak water.
The Titanic's lamps hang on its sides like fruit
on lit cliffs. We're shriven for rescue.

The sea snaps at our caulking.
We bend to our oars and praise God
and flex our fingers to bring
a drowned child out from the tarpaulin.

We're neither mothers nor fathers, but children,
fearful and full of trust,
lamblike as the Titanic goes down
entombing its witnesses.

We row on in a state of grace
in our half-empty lifeboats, sailing
westward for America, pilgrims,
numb to the summer-like choir
of fifteen hundred companions.

An Irish miner in Staffordshire

On smooth buttercup fields
the potholers sink down like dreams
close to Roman lead-mining country.

I sink the leafless shaft of an hydrangea twig
down through the slippy spaces I've made for it.
Dusted with hormone powder, moist,
its fibrous stem splays into root.

I graze the soft touches of compost
and wash them off easily, balled
under the thumb – clean dirt.
There's the man who gave me my Irish name

still going down, wifeless, that miner
who shafted the narrow cuffs of the earth
as if it was this he came for.

Code-breaking in the Garden of Eden

The Raw Garden is a collection of closely-related poems, which are intended to speak to, through, and even over each other. The poems draw their full effect from their setting; they feed from each other, even when the link is as mild as an echo of phrasing or cadence.

It is now possible to insert new genes into a chromosomal pattern. It is possible to feed in new genetic material, or to remove what is seen as faulty or damaged material. The basic genetic code is contained in DNA (deoxyribonucleic acid), and its molecular structure is the famous double helix, so called because it consists of two complementary spirals which match each other like the halves of a zip. Naturally-occurring enzymes can be used to split the double strand, and to insert new material. The separate strands are then recombined to form the complete DNA helix. By this process of gene-splicing a new piece of genetic information can be inserted into a living organism, and can be transmitted to the descendants of the organism.

It seems to me that there is an echo of this new and revolutionary scientific process in the way each poet feeds from the material drawn together in a long poetic tradition, "breaks" it with his or her individual creative voice, and recombines it through new poems.

One thing I have tried to do in these poems is to explore the effect which these new possibilities of genetic manipulation may have on our concept of what is natural and what is unnatural. If we can not follow Romantic poets in their assumption of a massive, unmalleable landscape which moulds the human creatures living upon it and provides them with a constant, stable frame of reference, then how do we look at landscape and at the "natural"? We are used to living in a profoundly human-made landscape. As I grew up I realised that even such apparently wild places as moors and commons were the product of human decisions and work: people had cut down trees, grazed animals, acquired legal rights. But still this knowledge did not interfere with my sense that these places were natural.

The question might be, what does it take to disturb the sense of naturalness held by the human being in his or her landscape? Is there a threshold beyond which a person revolts at a feeling that changedness has gone too far? Many of these poems focus on highly manipulated landscapes and outcrops of "nature", and on the harmonies and revulsions formed between them and the people living among them.

Perhaps the Garden of Eden embodies some yearning to print down an idea of the static and the predictable over our knowledge that we have to accept perpetual changeability. The code of the Garden of Eden has been broken open an infinite number of times. Now we are faced with a still greater potential for change, since we have acquired knowledge of the double helix structure of DNA. If the Garden of Eden really exists it does so moment by moment, fragmented and tough, cropping up like a fan of buddleia high up in the gutter of a deserted warehouse, or in a heap of frozen cabbages becoming luminous in the reflected light off roadside snow. This Garden of Eden propagates itself in strange ways, some of which find parallels in far-fetched horticultural techniques such as air layering, or growing potatoes in a mulch of rotted seaweed on white sand. I hope that these poems do not seem to hanker back to a prelapsarian state of grace. If I want to celebrate anything, it is resilience, adaptability, and the power of improvisation.

HELEN DUNMORE